Victorian Watercolours

RURAL LIFE

Victorian Watercolours
RURAL LIFE

ADRIAN VINCENT

Michael Joseph London

There is a wealth of Victorian watercolours available. Many were painted by artists who only produced a few paintings and little of their personal history is known. For this reason, it has not always been possible to find out the date of birth and death for all the artists shown in this book. 'Exhibited' gives the dates when an artist's work is known to have appeared in exhibitions. 'Flourished' gives the dates for the main body of an artist's work.

First published in Great Britain by Michael Joseph Ltd.
27 Wrights Lane, London W8
1987
© 1987 Beanstalk Books Ltd.
Produced by Beanstalk Books Ltd.,
89 Park Hill, London SW4 9NX

Designed by Lee Robinson

British Library Cataloguing in Publication Data

Vincent, Adrian
    Rural life. – (Victorian watercolours).
    1. Watercolor painting, British   2. Water-
    color painting, Victorian – Great Britain
    3. Country life in art
    I. Title   II. Series
    754   ND2365

ISBN 0-7181-2873-7

Printed in Great Britain by Purnell Book Production Limited

Acknowledgements
The assistance of the following art dealers and auctioneers in lending colour photographs for this book is gratefully acknowledged.

Bonhams (Auctioneers)
Montpelier Galleries,
Montpelier Street,
London SW7.

Fine-Lines (Fine Art)
The Old Rectory, 31 Ship St,
Shipston on Stour,
Warwick CV36 4AE.

Heather Newman
'Milidduwa', Mill Lane,
Cranham, Nr Painswick, Glos.

Phillips (Auctioneers)
Blenstock House, 7 Blenheim St,
New Bond St,
London W1Y OAS.

The Priory Gallery
The Priory, Station Rd,
Bishops Cleeve,
Cheltenham, Glos.

Contents

ROBERT THORNE WAITE

1842-1935

Robert Thorne Waite's long life spanned two generations of painters. It is therefore hardly surprising that his work shows three distinct styles which can be classified into early, middle and late phases but his hand always remains recognisable. He was a landscape artist whose work owed something to Copley Fielding and to that of his friend, Thomas Collier. Although the wealth of his detail is not immediately obvious, it is this particular aspect which often makes his work notable.

In his painting, *The End of the Day*, the shepherd and his dog are seen returning home from the day's work to be met, presumably by his wife, while the daughter opens the farm gates. By the subtle application of various coloured washes, the artist has managed to convey that the stream is flowing fast.

Because he is more concerned with depicting the overall scene, Thorne Waite's shepherd is almost a subordinate figure in the painting, his trade indicated only by the crook he is carrying. But then, rather oddly, the shepherd as central figure in a composition was not a popular subject with Victorian watercolour artists, even though he was a very important part of the rural landscape. Rather, it was the farm hands, waggoners and bucolic lads and lasses helping bring the harvest home – and even the sheep – who were their more commonplace subjects. But with a few exceptions, the shepherd and his way of life are hardly touched upon. There is the occasional hint that the shepherd's life was a harsh one, when the artist shows him, invariably as a distant figure, bringing his flock home through the snow in the darkening light, long after the ordinary labourer has gone home.

In many ways, the shepherd's life was a much harder one than that of the ordinary rural labourer. He was expected to work long hours on some bleak moor or windswept downs, with only his dog for company. At lambing time, between January and March, he lived for weeks on end, day and night, in a wheeled hut, seeing no one until the lambing time was over. Even after lambing, he was still liable to find himself out all night if there had been an outbreak of sheep-stealing – a crime generally carried out by organised bands working from towns and villages, whose perpetrators were quite prepared to use violence against the unlucky shepherd.

Thorne Waite, who was never happier than when spending time on the South Downs, must have seen many such shepherds while on his painting expeditions, but he always preferred to paint corn and hay fields.

Born in Cheltenham on 18 April 1842, he lived for a while in London but finally settled in Bournemouth, where he died in 1935.

The End of the Day
Courtesy The Priory Gallery

MYLES BIRKET FOSTER

1825-1899

Myles Birket Foster was a book illustrator and watercolour artist who enjoyed a great deal of success in his own lifetime. His reputation has grown steadily over the years, even though many may now find much of his work rather sentimental. Like a number of his contemporaries, he too was guilty of depicting a highly romanticised picture of rural England where well-scrubbed milkmaids, rosy-cheeked children and happy harvesters lived and worked in a forever sunny Eden – a setting far removed from the brutish realities of the Victorian farm labourer's life.

Like most watercolour artists, Birket Foster often used washes, but achieved his best effects by working with a fine brush, as dry as possible, finishing off most of his paintings with the stippling method. Although he tended to idealise his subjects, Birket Foster never used a professional model, dolled-up in some semi- appropriate 'costume'. His farm workers and children are the genuine article, wearing the clothes they put on to go out into the fields.

The Hayfield is a typical Birket Foster subject, showing his rural figures relaxing on a summer's afternoon rather than hard at work in the fields. As with all his work his style is immediately recognisable.

His superb craftsmanship and command of colour are equally in evidence in his watercolour, *Children Herding Sheep Through a Gate*, shown on the front cover. The figures of the man carrying kindling and the two little girls swinging on the gate, who give way to a long vista of field after field, are all meticulously executed.

As well as being a watercolour artist, he was also a talented wood engraver, etcher and painter in oils. The legacy he has left us is an important one as it embodies all that was best in the realm of Victorian watercolours.

Birket Foster was born in North Shields on 4 February 1825, the seventh child of a Quaker family, who claimed that he could draw before he could speak. Starting off his professional career by working for a well-known wood engraver named Ebenezer Landells, his very first work appeared in an issue of *Punch* dated 5 September 1844. In the following year, the *Illustrated London News* was first published, a magazine for which he produced a large body of work covering a wide range of subjects.

In 1859, he turned at last to watercolour painting, and within three years had become a regular exhibitor at the Royal Watercolour Society and the Royal Academy. Leaving London in 1861, he settled in Witley, Surrey. He died in Weybridge, Surrey in 1899.

The Hayfield
Courtesy The Priory Gallery

HELEN ALLINGHAM

1848-1926

Helen Allingham's paintings of country dwellings, rural, often tumbledown cottages set in a flowering wilderness, frequently show the influence of Birket Foster, although her work is notable for the subtle use of washes. But her watercolours have a different sort of charm. Unlike a large number of Victorian artists who liked to give an idealised picture of rural abodes, Allingham's cottages always looked lived in, with the thatch in a sad state of repair – as one might expect in the home of humble country people with no money to spare. *A Cottage Near Crewkerne* is typical of her work. Here a child occupies only a small portion of the watercolour, yet is so placed as to draw the eye irresistibly before it takes in the rest of the picture.

It was natural enough that Helen Allingham should like to paint country cottages surrounded by beautiful gardens. The country garden had always played an important part in rural life, providing people with a wide variety of flowers which were used for all manner of purposes. Honeysuckle gave food for goats, marigolds made a flavouring for broths, lavender was used to ward off house moths, and hollyhocks for making indigo dye.

Helen Allingham (*née* Paterson) was born near Burton-on-Trent, Derbyshire on 26 September 1848. She received her initial training as an artist at the Birmingham School of Design before going to London in 1867 in order to enter the Royal Academy Schools for Art.

Two years later she made the rounds of the publishers with a portfolio of her work – a practice almost unheard of in those days. Although there were a large number of other women artists working in this period, and while it was perfectly acceptable for them unobtrusively to take work to a gallery for exhibition, it was considered quite another matter for a woman to confront publishers almost daily in their offices. She had to deal with a male-dominated society, one which had not allowed women to become members of the Royal Academy Schools until 1860. It says much for the quality of her work that even in such an atmosphere she soon obtained commissions for book illustration – a fiercely competitive field already full of highly talented artists.

After gaining success as an illustrator, she moved on to the staff of the *Graphic*, where she met and married the Irish poet, William Allingham. Setting up house in Cheyne Walk, Chelsea, they soon became close friends of some of the Pre-Raphaelites and literary giants of the day, among them John Ruskin and Thomas Carlyle. In 1881 they moved to Witley, Surrey, where they were the near neighbours of Birket Foster. Now, with the Surrey countryside on her doorstep, Helen's talents were at last able to come into full flower. There she worked continually until her death.

A Cottage Near Crewkerne
Courtesy The Priory Gallery

THOMAS MacKAY

Flourished 1893-1913

Although Thomas MacKay has become a highly collectable artist, very little is known about him except that he exhibited at the Royal Academy on a few occasions. We know that he was a Liverpool man who had a studio at Littleton, Cheshire, from whence he made regular painting excursions into the countryside around Leamington and Warwick. From a brief appreciation of his work that appeared in the *Liverpool Courier* in 1913, it would seem that by then he had become something of a local celebrity, whose work had travelled to such far-flung places as Peru and Durban.

He flourished towards the close of the Victorian era, when much of the sentimentalism so dear to the painters of that period was being swept away. MacKay's paintings remained traditional in subject, though much of his work has a misty and poetic look to it which is almost Impressionistic. He was an artist who seems to have been fond of painting ducks, which appear so often in his work as to make one suspect they were added afterwards for decoration, rather than having been there while he sketched. MacKay's paintings give us a picture of a rural world of clean village streets and a gentle way of life which was certainly not the reality experienced by the farm hands.

In *Feeding the Ducks* we are clearly in the world of the gentry. The young woman was probably the wife or daughter of a village squire or landowner. In fact, the ruling classes have often been portrayed as the villains of the rural scene. William Cobbett, in his *Rural Rides* (1830) referred to the squirearchy as 'the most cruel, the most unfeeling, the most brutally insolent . . . the most base of all creatures that God has suffered to disgrace the human shape'.

Yet this was a one-sided view of the gentry. Many squires and landowners were conscious of their social responsibilities, some of them even going so far as to create model villages for their labourers. Such philanthropic gestures were based on the correct assumption that a well housed and well cared-for labour force was a more desirable asset than a discontented one. They subscribed to the upkeep of village schools, churches and reading rooms and generally tried to minister to the pastoral and physical needs of their tenants and labourers.

None of this, of course, affected MacKay's lady with her ducks. Cocooned in her comfortable world, she remains frozen in time by MacKay's brush, an attractive young woman who belonged to an era and a way of life that was swept away by the First World War.

Feeding the Ducks
Courtesy The Priory Gallery

DAVID COX

1783-1859

Generally acknowledged today as one of the leading masters of the British School of landscape painters, David Cox's work has been compared favourably with that of two other great masters, William Turner and Peter de Wint. With every brush stroke he was able to convey his passionate love of the English and Welsh countryside which he painted in a highly individual way, never stepping over the border into some fairyland of his own imagination. Always faithful to nature, he captured with equal ease the soothing airiness of the rural scene on a summer's day, or a landscape with lowering clouds heralding an approaching storm as it began to spread over the countryside. Even in the latter stages of his life, when he was also working in oils his work never lost its poetic feel for the countryside.

His *Figures and Cattle in a Wooded Landscape*, painted in Wales, is an excellent example of his work, a perfectly composed watercolour in which the strong colours used in the foreground for the trees, stream and gossiping women, gradually give way to the delicate washes used to indicate the more rugged terrain, culminating in mist shrouded mountains. The whole composition evokes a gracious and forever lost rural England.

David Cox was born on 29 April 1783, at Deritend, a suburb of Birmingham. Here he might well have lived and died in obscurity had he not stumbled over a door scraper when young and broken a leg, an accident that was to change his life. While he was laid up, a cousin gave him a paint box, a present which so delighted Cox that he began producing coloured copies of prints. These were sold to neighbours and friends of the family by his proud parents, who eventually sent him to a local drawing school.

Aside from his subsequent career as a watercolour artist, his life was uneventful, embracing a brief stint as an apprentice to a miniature artist, and another as a scene painter for the Theatre Royal, Birmingham, before he finally opted to become an art master. In 1841, and now an acknowledged master of his craft, he returned to his roots settling in Harborne, near Birmingham, where he died in 1859. He left behind him a large body of work, covering a wide range of subjects. But it is for his watercolours of the green lanes and quiet meadows of England and Wales that he will best be remembered.

Figures and Cattle in a Wooded Landscape
Courtesy Phillips

WILLIAM HENRY GORE

Flourished 1880-1920

William Henry Gore belongs to that small body of late Victorian painters who were able to carry on successfully the traditions of the early watercolour artists, while still painting in a way that was uniquely their own. He was a romantic painter who specialised in sentimental genre paintings. Gore's work is distinguished by the empathy with which he invariably executes a simple scene. The feeling with which he tackles his subject shows that here was an artist not merely catering for the Victorian public's seemingly insatiable demand for pretty, romantic pictures of the English countryside.

Gore's *Eventide* is a charming example of his work, in which he brings the two figures firmly into the foreground by giving everything around them a slightly misty look, one which is also in keeping with the time of day. We can tell from his clothes and scythe that here is a farm labourer returning from work. Is the woman his sweetheart? Have they met by chance? It is interesting to speculate.

The figures give the impression of a couple living in complete harmony with each other and the world around them. It was a view of rural people generally shared by urban Victorians, and had been aptly summed up a generation earlier by Oliver Goldsmith in a couplet from his poem, 'The Deserted Village' (1770):

His best companions, innocence and health;
And his best riches, ignorance of wealth.

Although Goldsmith's words may seem condescending now, there was then some truth in them. Despite the harsh conditions under which he often worked, the farm labourer knew that his lot was much better than that of his fellows forced to live in the towns. His working life was ten years' longer than that of his urban counterpart, and his children were able to grow up with the memory of summertimes spent in the fresh air, with the open countryside as their playground. If his wages were low, he could console himself with the fact that his money was often supplemented in kind, such as a weekly ration of beer or cider and wood and potatoes.

Those who had lived through and successfully weathered the age of rural decline (see page 22) had found that the labour shortage caused by the abandonment of the land by so many others, had finally led to higher wages. It is hardly surprising that many labourers who were interviewed at the turn of the century said that, looking back, they had been contented and well satisfied with their way of life.

Gore's work appeared in all the major London galleries and he also exhibited at the Royal Academy, where, over a short period, thirty-four pictures were shown. He lived for a while in London at 56 Princess Square, Kennington Park Road, and later at Newbury, Berkshire.

Eventide
Courtesy The Priory Gallery

HENRY JOHN SYLVESTER STANNARD

1870-1951

Henry John Sylvester Stannard was born in London on 12 July 1870, the son of Henry Stannard, a well known painter of landscape and sporting subjects, who lived long enough (1920) to see his son also become an established figure in the art world. The younger Stannard was a watercolour artist who specialised in painting rural landscapes and cottage gardens. Technically, his work often resembles that of Birket Foster. However, unlike Birket Foster, Stannard's work sometimes captures something of the rural decay that had begun in the second half of the nineteenth century. The realities of decline are nowhere in evidence even in the later work of Birket Foster who, in common with most other Victorian artists, preferred to opt for a sentimental and romanticised view of rural life.

The decay of rural England was sudden and dramatic. In 1851 there had been more than two million people working on the land, which had made it the largest single source of employment for England's workforce. But by the time Stannard had begun painting, great changes had already occurred in English rural life. Free trade and the rapid growth of industrialism – its factories and ugly workers' cottages spreading across much of the land – had supplanted agriculture from its role as the mainstay of the nation, with the result that many abandoned the land in favour of a better paid job in some factory. Those who remained, small farmer and labourer alike, struggled to survive in a landscape where the windmills and water mills had often stopped turning, and where bankrupt farms were being bought for a pittance or left to fall into ruin.

Something of this dark period in the history of rural England is reflected obliquely in Stannard's *A Rural Landscape*. The house seems derelict, the water wheel no longer turns. It is obviously occupied as smoke is rising from the chimney, a few chickens are scratching about and the little girl is sailing her boat on the pond. Stannard's flat, almost sombre lighting of the picture adds to the faint air of desolation that pervades the scene.

Although Stannard was born in London and received his art training in South Kensington, most of his life was spent in Bedfordshire, where he was an enthusiastic member of both the local operatic company and repertory theatre.

Stannard's work attracted the attention of several members of the Royal Household, including Queen Mary and the Duke of Windsor, who owned some of his watercolours. A frequent exhibitor at the Royal Academy, Stannard is also known for his occasional use of the split brush technique. Here the bristles are split to achieve a more precise look to the detail in a painting, a technique which had been pioneered by the artist John Glover (see page 40).

A Rural Landscape
Courtesy Phillips

JAMES JACKSON CURNOCK

1839–1891

James Jackson Curnock was a Bristol landscape artist who was taught to paint by his father, James Curnock, a genre and portrait artist of some repute whose work is to be found in the Bristol Art Gallery. It is the son, however, who is the better-known artist. He was first brought to the attention of the public by John Ruskin, who referred to *The Llugwy at Capel Curig* as being 'skilful and affectionate to a high degree' (Academy Notes 1875). It is an appraisal which could be applied to almost all his work.

His watercolour, *Near Capel Curig*, was painted at a famous beauty spot in Wales which many other watercolour artists had visited, including Thomas Collier and David Cox, attracted by its beautiful walks and arctic and alpine flowers. Nestling under the shadow of Snowdonia, it had the added advantage of being a place where artists could paint in peace, being a remote area and seldom visited by sightseers during the nineteenth century.

Curnock's beautiful and tranquil study of a woman and her son using stepping stones to cross a stream is painted rather in the manner of David Cox, with a great deal of detail to be seen in the foreground, before the eye is carried on past the corn stooks to a farmhouse and a man tying a cover over a hayrick, and then on again to the distant hills and the beginning of the mountain range. The right-hand side of the picture also repays study, for the detail of the trees with the odd patch of sunlight filtering through the ferns beneath, and the lily pads seen floating just beneath the surface of the waters. The picture was painted between 1873 and 1874, and was sold for eight guineas at the time. Today it would fetch nearly a hundred times that amount.

As with all watercolour artists who went to Wales, Curnock's paintings give no hint that this was an unhappy land ruled mostly by rapacious land agents who were continually putting up the rents, and callous land owners forever evicting those who could not pay. In fact, most of the fault lay at the door of the land agents, who were often acting for absentee and indifferent landlords. Finding themselves with almost unlimited powers that included being able to shorten leases and enclose land previously available to the small farmer, they became despotic tyrants who literally terrorised whole areas, eventually leading to the farm labourers' riots of the 1850s and 1860s. It is, therefore, hardly surprising that there was a steady emigration from Wales which lasted right up until 1911.

James Jackson Curnock was born in 1839. He was living at 7 Richmond Hill, Clifton, Bristol at the time of his death in 1891. Towards the end of his life he began painting in oils. His work is to be found in the Bristol Art Gallery.

Near Capel Curig

Courtesy Fine-Lines (Fine Art)

JOSEPH KIRKPATRICK

Born 1872

Joseph Kirkpatrick was a Liverpool engraver and artist who was fortunate enough to have studied under three good teachers, first with John Finnie, who exhibited at the Royal Academy for more than forty years, and then at the Academie Julian in Paris under William Adolphe Bouguerau and Gabriel Ferrier, two famous artists of their day.

A landscape and genre artist who liked to show humble farm people at work – women picking potatoes or men ploughing or harrowing – his work sometimes has an earthy quality about it which distances it from much of what was being painted around that time.

Kirkpatrick's *Harrowing* was painted after the harvest had been gathered in and the ricks set. Now the time had come to prepare the land for another crop or to let it lie fallow for a while. The farmer (or his man) has hitched the harrow behind his team of two Shire horses. Ahead of him lies a hard day of monotonous work. But unlike the modern farmer sitting in the cabin of his tractor, isolated from the sun or breeze, his forebear was out in the fresh air with the breeze on his cheeks, accompanied by his horses and his ears filled with bird song. Sometimes, just sometimes, the conditions under which the Victorian farm hand worked were better than those of his modern counterpart.

On a first examination, Kirkpatrick's choice of subject may seem an odd one. An ugly-looking contraption being pulled by two horses does not have the same instant appeal of a ploughman following two Shire horses. The horses are not even painted in profile, which would have given him a pleasant but uninspired angle, but instead he has chosen to depict them with their hindquarters towards us and, moreover, well over to the right of the painting, leaving a wide vista of earth to dominate the picture.

We can speculate as to the reasons why the artist has chosen this interesting perspective. Maybe it is to emphasise the sense of unglamorous work; maybe it is to make us aware of the red earth stretching far beyond. Set in a lonely landscape, and highlighting an agricultural implement which has been used in one form or another since man first began farming, it is a picture that must be ranked among Kirkpatrick's best work.

Harrowing
Courtesy Fine-Lines (Fine Art)

GEORGE O. OWEN

Exhibited 1887-1926

George Owen was a Midlands watercolour artist from Birmingham who painted genre and landscape subjects which were exhibited mainly at the Royal Birmingham Society of Artists between 1887 and 1926. His work covered a wide range of subjects including attractive landscape scenes, often showing farm labourers at work, and seascapes. Although he also lived in Tewkesbury and Old Trafford, Manchester, his loyalties always remained with Birmingham, where an exhibition of one hundred of his paintings was held posthumously.

Owen's *Homeward* was painted towards the end of the Victorian age, though in manner and style it could have been executed during the earlier Romantic period in watercolour painting. A well-composed and rather striking picture, it was done at a time when the public conscience had been awakened by the various pieces of legislation which had recently been implemented to improve the farm labourer's lot. A glimmer of this new awareness of the hardships farm labourers had to endure is reflected in Owen's painting. His workers look tired, especially the women, and there is not a smiling face among them. Even the horse looks dispirited. It could have been a rather melancholy picture, but it is saved from being so by the wonderful use of light, with the last of the afternoon sun bathing important areas of the scene.

In common with most farm workers, Owen's farm hands would almost certainly have been taken on at a Hiring Fair, an annual event at which the farm workers presented themselves dressed in their Sunday best, with a badge of their craft in their lapel. If they were fortunate enough to be hired, their agreement would include a fixed wage, board and lodgings. A brief but good description of a Hiring Fair can be found in chapter six of Thomas Hardy's *Far From the Madding Crowd*.

Those with a family to support were more likely to consult local newspaper advertisements, inserted by farmers hoping to get a 'package deal' from a labourer looking for employment and board, not only for himself but also for other family members.

In Northumberland and Durham, the situation was even worse as the farmers in those areas operated the 'bondage' system, in which a labourer could not get employment *unless* he supplied also a female labourer as part of an annual contract. This form of servitude continued almost to the beginning of the twentieth century.

Homeward
Courtesy The Priory Gallery

THOMAS JAMES LLOYD

1849-1910

While there is a constant re-appraisal of the works of the Victorian watercolour artists, with the status of some inevitably falling under rigorous scrutiny, Thomas James Lloyd is one whose reputation has particularly soared. Primarily a landscape artist who also painted genre and marine subjects, his work attracted critical acclaim as soon as he began exhibiting in 1870. From the beginning he was seen as an artist whose subtle use of colour and method of composition entitled him to be ranked among the greatest of the English landscape painters. Time and changing tastes have done nothing to detract from that opinion.

His rural scenes, often of a country garden or river bank, generally graced by the presence of an elegant young woman taking a stroll on a summer's day with her little daughter, are so distinctive in their style as to make them instantly recognisable.

His watercolour, *Lilacs*, was probably painted in one of those country gardens which could be found in every corner of Victorian rural England. In this case, Lloyd had set up his easel in the garden of a member of the gentry, if the woman's dress and hair style are anything to go by. As with all Lloyd's work, this charming study is full of small details. Everywhere there are spring flowers – white carnations, wallflowers, and even a few shy violets almost under the woman's feet, as well as buttercups and daisies in profusion. They are all painted with the lightest touch.

buttercups and daisies in profusion. They are all painted with the lightest touch.

The tumbledown cottage beyond the gate presumably belonged to the family and was, no doubt, occupied by someone working for them – its shabby proximity would never otherwise have been tolerated.

Even if the style of the woman's light cotton dress had not told us that the picture was painted during the latter part of the nineteenth century, the garden would have provided a clue. For it was around this time that the gentry began remodelling their gardens, replacing their Italianate terraces and sweeping lawns studded with statuary with something far simpler. They banished exotic plants brought from around the world and replaced them with borders full of the sort of hardy English perennials commonly found in their labourer's country cottage garden.

Little is known about Thomas Lloyd's personal life except that he was born in London in 1849, and that he lived at several addresses, including Walmer in Kent, and Yapton in Sussex. He died in 1910. He is more commonly known as Tom Lloyd.

Lilacs
Courtesy The Priory Gallery

GEORGE FREDERICK NICHOLLS

Exhibited 1885-1937

George Frederick Nicholls was a landscape and flower painter who was living in Liverpool when he first began exhibiting in 1885. Later, he moved to a number of other places, mostly in Cheshire and Worcester. But his heart lay in the Cotswolds, to which he returned to paint time after time, eventually becoming so well known as a painter of that area as to be commissioned to supply the illustrations for a book called *The Cotswolds* (1908). He exhibited at the Royal Academy on several occasions but most of his work was shown at the Walker Gallery in London.

One of the main elements of a successful watercolour is the way the artist manages to use his washes so that his paper is not merely a surface, but also a collaborator, showing through the lighter tones of the watercolour to give an overall fluid look to his work. In his painting, *Gloucestershire Village,* George Nicholls demonstrates the point in the way he uses his washes thinly in many areas of the picture for example on the walls of the houses. For the trees and other areas of green, the colour is applied more solidly to give body to the picture. Within the bounds of the technique Nicholls has used, the subject is treated realistically and is full of informative little details, like the glimpse of lilac seen through the trees which tells us that it is early summer. This is a real village, shown truly without undue straining for effect.

Nicholls' Gloucestershire village was just one of the countless little villages that gradually came into being during the eighteenth and nineteenth centuries, often the inadvertent creation of some farmer or squire who had built a few cottages for his workers. These were added to over the years until a whole complex of houses sprung up, generally around a parish church. As the village expanded the rural craftsmen arrived and set up in business, helping to create what was to become a close-knit community whose interdependence was almost total. Their lives were generally ruled by the squire and the local parson and the whole rhythm of the village was bound up with the seasons of ploughing, sowing and harvesting.

In this picture we can see wattle and daub buildings in which hazel twigs were interwoven between the timbers, daubed with clay reinforced with horsehair and then surfaced inside and out with a coat of plaster.

Thatching was a technique widely used for roofing because it kept the house warm in winter and cool in summer and could be adapted to fit almost any shape of roof. The fact that the windows were always small was of no concern to their inhabitants. They had no desire to see the sun streaming into their rooms because they worked outdoors all day. And as for the absence of a view, they had only to walk outside the village to feast their eyes on meadows and a countryside often stretching as far as the eye could see.

Gloucestershire Village
Courtesy The Priory Gallery

FREDERICK WILLIAMSON

Flourished 1856-1900

Victorian artists frequently chose to depict cattle as the focal point of their rural landscapes. One of the most prominent exponents of this genre was Frederick Williamson, whose work often had as subject cattle and sheep at pasture. Typical of this mode is *Cattle Grazing on Shanklin, Isle of Wight* which shows Ayrshire cows immediately recognisable by the shape of their horns. Since it was impossible to ship this breed to the Isle of Wight until 1820, when the first regular steamship began, the work cannot pre-date this time.

Williamson's painting of the cattle in this picture could not be bettered. As George Stubbs with horses, so Williamson had obviously made a close study of cattle, even though he did not go as far as putting them on the dissecting table, as Stubbs had done. Every muscle, every bony protuberance, every rib and sinew are clearly defined. Even the stance of the standing cow is exactly right. So perfect is their execution that one is hardly conscious at first of the sheep which share their pasture.

Perhaps Williamson's interest in cattle grew to be an obsession because he was fortunate enough to have been painting at a time when breeds of all kinds were making their first appearance in every corner of the British Isles.

Frederick Williamson's early work was done very much in the Pre-Raphaelite style, and then suddenly he switched to becoming a traditional landscape painter. He was a regular exhibitor at the Royal Academy and all the major galleries from 1856 to 1900.

Originally a Londoner from Islington, where he lived in Goswell Road, he later moved to Farncombe Villas, Godalming, where he painted a number of local scenes. Four years later, in 1870, he moved again, this time to Vine Cottage, in the nearby village of Witley, where he must have met Helen Allingham and Birket Foster. The latter had bought a charming, ivy cottage there called Tigbourne in 1862. Even so, Williamson does not seem to have come under their influence as he continued to paint very much in his usual style, with the emphasis on cattle scenes.

The move seems to have been a beneficial one from a financial point of view, as it was from this date that the prices he obtained for his pictures began to double to around twenty pounds. If this still seems a modest sum, it was a better rate of payment than was obtained by most members of the Royal Society of British Artists, of which Williamson was a member.

Williamson exhibited at many of the major galleries, including the Royal Academy, where he showed thirty seven pictures. One hundred and fifteen of his pictures are known to have survived including *Sheep with Lambs, A Cow and Sheep* and *Sheep at Rest*.

Cattle Grazing on Shanklin, Isle of Wight
Courtesy Fine-Lines (Fine Art)

AUGUSTUS WALFORD WEEDON

1838-1908

Although not ranked among the major watercolour artists, Augustus Walford Weedon has always been considered a very competent painter whose relaxed style has a pleasing simplicity about it which is often very soothing to look at. Born in London in 1838, Weedon was a landscape artist who travelled and painted widely in England, Scotland and Wales, and who was already exhibiting at the Royal Academy by the time he was twenty-one. From then until he finished showing his work to the public in 1892, he painted two hundred and sixty-nine watercolours, covering a wide range of subjects from a view of a Highland Glen to fishing smacks off Rye, in Sussex.

His watercolour, *Harvesters at Lunch*, is a good example of his work. The confident and competent way in which he has painted a large expanse of sky serves to enhance rather than detract from what is going on in the fields below. Although the landscape is depicted on a small scale compared to the sky, every minute detail is there. The harvest is in, leaving only the stubble, and the harvesters are settling down to their lunch, their pitchforks seen embedded in the earth behind them. Weedon painted this picture in the 1890s at a time when most farm labourers were better fed than they had been some forty years earlier. Weedon's harvesters had probably breakfasted on porridge, with tea and bread and butter, and had then gone off with a hunk of bread and some cheese in their pocket for lunch. In the evening, they would return to a supper of meat and vegetables – a luxury compared to the mid-nineteenth century when any farm hand could count himself very lucky if he had meat more than three times a week.

Not that things had improved in other areas. The farm labourer's life was still one of unremitting toil, with harvest time being the worst period of all, with its usual annual quota of deaths or hideous wounds, generally viewed with scant sympathy by the farm owners.

Weedon and his work belong to that transitional period in Victorian art when many other painters were forming break-away groups in order to imbue their work with a new-found social realism. In the process, they discarded all the old Romanticism in art that had catered for the great urban nostalgia for a past which had never really existed, but which so many other artists had fostered. Weedon was in no sense a revolutionary. He recorded exactly what he saw, without any social comment, and in doing so made a valuable contribution to the infinite number of styles and variety of subject matter that make the study of Victorian watercolours so fascinating.

Harvesters at Lunch

Courtesy Bonhams

WILLIAM W. GOSLING

1824-1883

A prolific artist with the habit of titling many of his pictures with a pretentious poetic quotation, William Gosling was, nevertheless, very talented and capable of painting a highly charged, atmospheric picture. A well-regarded painter who specialised in large landscape and rustic genre paintings, his work was so popular with the public that the impending arrival of a new work by him at an exhibition was an event eagerly awaited. As one might expect from an artist who produced two hundred and seventeen known works, the quality of his paintings vary. But at its best, his work matches anything that was done by Thomas Collier, considered by many to be the supreme English watercolour artist of his time. Gosling painted a wide range of rural subjects, and much of his work was done around the middle Thames countryside. Born in London in 1824, he had a highly successful career.

Gosling's watercolour, *Sheep on the Downs*, shows him at his best. This study of a large flock of sheep browsing among the wild bracken and gorse on some lonely part of the Downs is very powerful with its threatening, dark rolling clouds and the flocks of birds wheeling in the sky. It is executed very much in the early nineteenth-century manner.

Although the young girl and child helping to tend the sheep are only lightly depicted, the rest of the scene is executed in a richly detailed manner, with some fine brush work being used for the sheep and bracken.

From the printed lists and catalogues that exist of Gosling's work, we know that he was fond of painting sheep but, as with all the Victorian artists, he seemed reluctant to show the shepherd as anything but a distant figure. His interest lay with the sheep themselves – in trying to capture with his brush the texture of their wool, or in using them merely as ornamental additions to a scene.

This lack of interest in shepherds seems to have been shared by nearly all the nineteenth century recorders of the English rural scene. The omission is surprising as the shepherd was an important member of the community.

The shepherd, with his specialised skills, was an invaluable asset to the farmer. The shepherd could recognise when a sheep was ailing – often by the droop of its ear or the way it twitched its tail. The farmer asked the shepherd's advice when they went to market together and the shepherd would point out any animal that could be suffering from one of the many ailments common to sheep.

Sheep on the Downs
Courtesy The Priory Gallery

JOHN GLOVER

1767-1849

Aside from his standing as a watercolour artist of considerable importance, John Glover was one of those very rare instances of a nineteenth-century painter whose life and personality were even more interesting than his work.

An enormous man weighing nearly twenty stone and afflicted with two club feet, he was still able to move around the countryside on painting expeditions in England, Scotland and Wales. He had great energy and amongst his many other activities he managed to be a highly successful drawing master, bird tamer and student of animals in general. At the age of sixty-three he capped his flamboyant career by becoming the first English artist of any note to settle in Australia.

The son of a farmer, Glover was born in 1767, at Houghton-on-the-Hill, Leicestershire, where, in his youth, he worked for his father on the land. At first largely self-taught, he later became a writing master at a school in Appleby and then a drawing master in Litchfield. He began to exhibit at the Royal Academy in 1795, as well as to hold a series of one-man exhibitions, while still running his own drawing school. At the height of his success he decided to emigrate to Australia and, in 1831, settled on a large estate in Tasmania, which he called 'Patterdale' after one of his favourite spots on Lake Ullswater, Cumberland. From there he continued to send his work to London for exhibition until his death in 1849, at the age of eighty-two.

Straddling the time from William Turner's domination of British art, to the beginning of the mid-Victorian period of English watercolours, his style belongs to that earlier period when artists were more interested in laying down a scene, rather than peopling it with rural characters. His work, mostly large in size, was therefore rather lacking in human interest, consisting mostly of empty sylvan scenes or architectural views. Often dark-toned and generally deficient in colour, much of his work is still distinguished by the fine detail of his brush work when he painted foliage, achieved by the split brush technique which he invented (see page 22), and for the way he dampened his paper to achieve a soft effect with his washes. His style was greatly influenced by that of the French artist, Claude Lorrain, a seventeenth-century artist and engraver, whose work he admired so much that he went to the length of selling the house he was then occupying in Ullswater to buy just one of his pictures!

His watercolour, *A Mill in Bonsall Dale, Derbyshire*, is a typical example of his work. An accomplished and highly detailed watercolour which captures something of the bleakness of parts of the Derbyshire Dales, it also displays the splendid effects that Glover was able to achieve when painting trees by his split brush technique.

A Mill in Bonsall Dale, Derbyshire
Courtesy Bonhams

DAVID ROBERTSON

Exhibited 1883-1894

The era of Victorian watercolours abounds with the names of talented artists who managed to achieve a certain measure of success only to sink into sudden obscurity. David Robertson must be numbered among them. A landscape artist who lived in Edinburgh and then in Douglas on the Isle of Man, he exhibited a number of times at the Scottish Royal Academy and the Royal Academy in London, but after 1894 was heard of no more.

His *Sheep in the Snow*, which was probably painted in Scotland, is an evocative painting which repays close and imaginative scrutiny by the viewer. It is a picture of a desolate, snow-locked landscape, where the silence is likely to be broken only by the sound of the wind. A darkening sun has appeared, but is about to set behind the trees, leaving the shepherd to the darkness of a bitterly cold night to be spent in his hut. Executed with a sure hand, it gives an idea of just how hard a shepherd's life could be.

Although the shepherd's life was characterised by long hours and almost permanent poverty, it did have its compensations. As a highly skilled and respected member of the community, whose employer depended on him for the welfare of valuable sheep, he was paid slightly more than the average farm worker. In addition, he received six pence for every lamb he reared, which was paid after the lambs had been sold. And there were other perks. He was allowed two bushels of malt during lamb-ing, and for every sheep he slaughtered he was entitled to *hid and pluck*, the head and the liver, which he put in a pot to make a stew, often supplemented with what he had managed to obtain on occasional poaching expeditions.

Everything the shepherd wore was traditional. His smock, or *slop*, was made from twilled linen and had no opening to it, either at back or front, but it did have two 'poacher's' pockets, which its elaborate smocking on the front had been designed to conceal. His boots were known as *shummackers*. These had flaps over the lace holes to keep out the water, and were made of a stout leather. His crook was made either from iron or hazel wood and was an implement which he used with considerable dexterity. With it, he could hook a sheep to him or, with a quick twist of the wrist, turn the animal over on its back.

Among the other essentials of his trade were the sheep bells he strung around their necks to help him locate his flock or any stray sheep lost in the autumnal mists. He had too a turnip pick and a beet chopper for breaking and cutting up food for his fold and a box of tar to smear on his sheeps' cuts and grazes. Less necessary but none the less important for maintaining his status in the community were the sleeved waistcoat, breeches and tall felt hat he wore for special occasions.

Sheep in the Snow
Courtesy Fine-Lines (Fine Art)

WALTER GOODALL

1830-1899

Walter Goodall was the youngest of three brothers whose father was a well-known engraver. His two brothers, Edward and Frederick, also became artists. However, it was Walter's misfortune to have his career suddenly blighted in 1875, when he became partially paralysed, a condition that gradually worsened until he became completely helpless.

Born in London in 1830, he received his training at the Royal Academy Schools, and thereafter worked entirely in watercolours. He produced some one hundred and fifty-nine paintings, including three that were shown at the Royal Academy, before he was forced to give up painting in 1884. His work was notable for the refinement of its execution, though there were times when he tended to sentimentalise his subjects, which were mostly peasant characters. Before his illness he travelled to Holland, Britanny, the Pyrenees and to Venice, where he painted a number of gondola scenes.

Goodall's painting, *The Gleaners*, shows a woman and her children returning home after gathering some of the ears of corn left by the reapers, which she would grind to make flour. Traditionally, a task done by the poorest of the poor since Biblical times, it was a subject immortalised by another picture of the same title by Millet, himself a humble peasant, whose work was to influence many of the Victorian painters. Goodall's gleaners and the general background are rendered very much in the manner of the early nineteenth-century artists. Its formalised style, with its use of hard lines and subdued colour, makes it look rather like an engraving – possibly showing the influence of his father's work. The fine detail which is to be found in every area of the picture shows a meticulous craftsmanship.

Gleaners like those in Goodall's picture were the last workers in a chain who began their task when a price had been settled between the farmer and the man he was to employ to bring in the harvest. After the deal had been struck, there followed a day of relaxation, spent partly at the blacksmith, sharpening the scythes and getting the blades set at the right angle in the shaft, while the remaining hours were passed in the ale house.

The next day the men would begin cutting their way through the corn, working in line across the fields, while the women followed behind, scooping up the sheaves. The gleaners gathered any corn the reapers had left. When the job was finally finished, the last sheaf of corn was always plaited into a *dolly* and taken into the house.

But the bringing in of the harvest did not end there. First the corn had to be dried and then skilfully stacked, otherwise it might rot or even catch light. All this was followed by a harvest holiday and a harvest supper supplied by the farmer – to which the unfortunate gleaners were not invited.

The Gleaners

Courtesy Heather Newman

HENRY JOHN KINNAIRD

Flourished 1880-1920

Henry John Kinnaird was a landscape artist who painted in a loose but still realistic style, mostly around Essex and Sussex. Originally a Londoner who lived off the Camden Road and then in Kentish Town, he moved eventually to Ringmer, near Lewes, Sussex, where he seems to have spent the rest of his life. He exhibited nine times at the Royal Academy, and at least one of his watercolours, *Summer*, reached America where it was shown at an exhibition in New York in 1902.

Kinnaird's *A Lane Near Pulborough* is an attractive watercolour which incorporates in a single picture all the rural elements likely to appeal to a landscape artist of the Victorian period. There are wandering sheep followed by the shepherd and his dog, farm hands bringing in the harvest, graceful trees and a distant rolling landscape. There is even the almost obligatory tumbledown cottage; it appears so often in this type of picture that Lord Tennyson was once prompted to ask Birket Foster why painters always preferred a tumbledown cottage. This brought the response, 'Because no-one likes a straight line'.

Despite the variety of detail to be found in the picture, the composition manages to bring all the elements together into a satisfying whole, with the trees on the left acting as a counterbalance to the cottage on the right.

Like so many other watercolours, it gives an idyllic picture of the countryside not always borne out by the often harsh economic conditions that prevailed. In fact, much grazing land was lost when many farmers began to obey the government's plea for them to grow more wheat.

Further loss of land occurred when vast areas were requisitioned to build reservoirs, forcing both the sheep and cattle farmers to evacuate their former lands. In addition, other areas were put aside for the preservation of game for the leisured shooting parties of the gentry. From 1870 until the turn of the century, England and Wales lost three million acres. In the same period, the number of sheep kept in those areas was drastically reduced.

A Lane Near Pulborough

Courtesy The Priory Gallery

CHARLES EARLE

1832-1893

Like so many Victorian watercolour artists, Charles Earle was a Londoner whose initial discovery of the countryside prompted him to spend much of his life exploring the high-ways and by-ways of rural Britain in a constant search for some new visual delight to share with his viewers. His artistic success can be measured in many of the two hundred and seventy-two paintings he left behind. Although a number of these were painted during his travels abroad in France, Germany and Italy, the main body of his work was of the English and Welsh countryside which he always painted with a lyrical feeling not always matched by some of his more famous contemporaries working in the same medium.

Born in London in 1832, Earle established his reputation as a watercolour artist when his work began to appear at the Royal Academy and elsewhere from 1857. He continued to exhibit until 1893, the year of his death in London.

His watercolour, *In the Canterbury Meadows*, is Earle at his best – a wonderfully detailed and lovingly painted picture which captures the feeling of tranquillity and beauty peculiar only to the English countryside at certain times of the year. The gnarled trees lining one side of the river walk, the cattle grazing in the distant pastures, the early morning mist still hanging over the trees and meadows, even the small figures of two men who have come to fish in the stream meandering through the rushes, all combine to make it a very pleasing picture.

Earle painted *In the Canterbury Meadows* in 1876, just before urban expansion had begun in earnest; a time therefore when one could still step out of a house in a provincial city such as Canterbury and, after only a short walk, find oneself in open fields. The area around Canterbury itself was spared any form of industrial growth for a long time for a number of reasons. Apart from being a cathedral city, Canterbury was a place where Hiring Fairs were held and, more importantly, it was a major centre in Kent for agricultural shows. Here farm workers, like the sheep shearers and ploughmen, could demonstrate their skills and farmers show off their prime livestock, with prizes given by manufacturers who used the fairs as a show place for their goods. All this made Canterbury and its environs a rural stronghold.

These agricultural shows, controlled by farmers' societies and numbering nearly a hundred across the country in 1835, helped to check the decline of many of the rural crafts, and actually halted the march of industrialisation in certain areas, right up to the beginning of the twentieth century.

In the Canterbury Meadows

Courtesy Bonhams

ARTHUR WINTER SHAW

Born 1869

A landscape watercolour artist who was fond of painting cattle, Arthur Winter Shaw was born in London in 1869. Originally a pupil at the Slade School, he lived in Peckham before moving to a number of other addresses in Kent and Sussex. As is true for the work of so many artists who were continually on the move, it is difficult to identify the exact spot where many of Shaw's pictures were painted. He exhibited from 1891 right up to 1936, but only seems to have shown two pictures at the Royal Academy.

Unlike many other artists of the period who were fond of painting highly detailed pictures in strong colours, Shaw used pale washes which give many of his works a pleasingly luminous effect. This is very much in evidence in his picture, *Summer*, where his use of pale washes presages the work of more modern painters. To a layman, parts of this watercolour may seem rather casually executed – the clump of four trees in the background appears to have been dabbed in as an afterthought. Yet they serve a definite purpose, helping to establish the boundary line where the fields end and the hills beyond begin.

The same seemingly casual treatment has been used to a slightly lesser degree on the cattle. But see how real they look. These are not the idealised cows we see in many paintings, their hides gleaming and the animals looking as if they have been cleaned up for an agricultural show. These cows with their underfed and generally uncared-for look would never have won any prizes. They are livestock one might well expect to see belonging to a small farmer forced to graze his cattle on poor land, rather than in the sort of rich pasture owned by the more well-to-do farmer. The girl who tends them is more strongly outlined so becoming the focal point in a picture which achieves its considerable effects by understatement.

For a long time, the job of tending cattle was considered women's work in many areas, beneath the dignity of the farm hand who would do it only if no other work was available. But by the time this picture was painted, the situation had already begun to change. Factories were beginning to spring up outside many of the towns, offering work for any woman who was prepared to walk a few miles into town and back. For someone who had been forced to work in the fields in all weathers, the lure of the factories must have been irresistible.

Summer
Courtesy The Priory Gallery

CARLETON GRANT

Exhibited 1885-1899

A landscape painter originally from Liverpool, Carleton Grant is one of those Victorian artists about whom we know little, possibly because his output was relatively small. However, this does not justify his neglect as he was an excellent artist painting in a near Impressionistic manner. He exhibited ten landscapes at the Royal Academy between 1892 and 1897, and then rather dropped from sight, though a few of his pictures continued to turn up sporadically over the next two years. He moved house frequently, living in Cheshire, Buckinghamshire and at Rhyl in North Wales. All his painting was done in the Thames Valley and North Wales.

His *Children Fishing at Dusk* is an arresting work executed in almost monochrome colours, where nothing very much seems to be going on, but which is, nevertheless, packed with atmospheric detail. The water of the lily pond is oily from the aftermath of a long, hot summer and undisturbed as yet by any rains that would have freshened it. The lily pads are turning brown on the surface and a few early autumnal leaves have drifted onto the stagnant surface from the overhanging elms. The little boy and girl are intent on catching tiddlers and quite oblivious of the young woman standing nearby – perhaps a servant girl waiting for her lover? It is early autumn, too early for heavy clothes, but with a feeling that indicates the colder days to come.

The colour is both painstakingly chosen and applied to excellent effect, the light on the water giving it a beautiful pearl-like sheen, while the bold use of various shades of brown blending into a harmonious whole is done with a deft and lively touch, which only a confident artist is capable of achieving.

Carleton Grant's picture depicts one of the backwaters of the Thames Valley and is not one painted in the 'heart of rural England'. But it was still part of the English countryside, just far enough away from the bustle and ugliness of urban life to make it an area where nature in all its glory could still be enjoyed.

Grant's painting is one that must evoke the same emotional response from everyone who has been in the country on an autumnal day, when the whole atmosphere seems tinged with that faint air of melancholy that is peculiar to the English countryside. It is far more tightly painted than most of his work in which he often used pale washes.

Carlton Grant painted many fine pictures, but as a 'mood' piece this must surely be rated as one of his best works.

Children Fishing at Dusk

Courtesy Fine-Lines (Fine Art)

CHARLES JAMES ADAMS

1859-1931

Charles James Adams was a landscape artist working in both oils and watercolours. Although born in Gravesend, he spent the early part of his life in Leicester before moving to Surrey, a county which seems to have held a particular attraction for many of the Victorian artists. A pupil of Wilmot Pilsbury who painted in the manner of Helen Allingham, he also produced genre and historical subjects as well as a number of lithographs during the early part of his career. His main output was in oils, but his watercolours are so finely executed as to make one wish that he had painted more often in this medium.

His watercolour, *Homeward*, is a vigorous example of his work, so boldly painted that from a distance it could be taken for an oil. It is a naturalistic picture in the best sense of the word, realistic without looking photographic, with everything clearly depicted, without the slightest element of fudging in any area, even down to the small brasses on the horses' foreheads, set there to ward off evil spirits. These four Shire horses being brought home from the fields were painted in the late afternoon of an autumn day, as we can see from the light, and the russet leaves clinging tenaciously to the tree in the foreground. It was painted at the beginning of the ploughing season which frequently carried on almost until Christmas.

The ploughmen were the elite of the rural labouring classes, and with good cause, as they needed a great deal of skill to 'cut a field out' – the ploughman had to divide the land into equal sections, separated by furrows. On land that was easily drained, twenty-two yards was the usual width, with five yards for less easily drained terrain. It was all hard, exacting work. Then, at the end of the day, the horses were watered and fed, the harnesses cleaned and waxed to preserve their suppleness and the brasses rubbed and burnished. Only when all this had been done could the ploughman return at last wearily home.

Mechanisation, with the inevitable job losses it brought in train, was naturally enough the enemy of all the rural labouring classes. The ploughmen were deeply antagonistic towards it and their strong affection for their horses was an important factor in their bitter opposition. Feelings ran so high in East Anglia that ploughmen made frequent attacks on the farms where they had once worked, destroying any new machinery that had been brought in.

Mechanisation affected not only the ploughmen but also the wheelwrights, blacksmiths and all the other rural craftsmen whose fortunes had been bound up with working horses. But the greatest loss were the horses themselves. With their departure from the fields of Britain a part of the old rural life of the country disappeared which could never be replaced.

Homeward
Courtesy The Priory Gallery

ROBERT GUSTAV MEYERHEIM

1847-1920

During the Victorian period quite a number of foreign artists came over from the Continent and settled in Britain. But few managed to gain the same 'feel' for the English countryside as Robert Meyerheim, whose rapidly acquired affinity for the English rural landscape became so strong that he was eventually able to hold an exhibition of his work in London, called *The Soul of the English Countryside*. The exhibition brought him considerable attention and led to a reviewer describing his works as '. . . wholly English in their conception, feeling and execution, and show the sweetness and charm of the countryside with an intimacy of perception that is vouchsafed to few'. This may be somewhat over effusive, as were most art reviewers in those days, but it does indicate that the critics had not failed to observe that Meyerheim was more English than the English when it came to painting a rural scene.

Mayerheim was originally a German landscape artist who was born in Danzig in 1847. After studying at the Düsseldorf Academy, he came to London in 1875, and almost immediately began exhibiting at the Royal Academy. A landscape and genre artist, he achieved his pleasing results by the relaxed and sensitive way he applied his washes with only the occasional use of a hard line. His work is often distinguished by the sense of immediacy he gives to a picture. With his charming watercolour, *Feeding the Calves*, one has the feeling that the painting was probably done on the spot, at one sit-ting, rather than having been 'worked up' from a number of sketches – though this was unlikely as the painting is a large one which could hardly have been completed in a single day.

Meyerheim's watercolour of a young girl in a hooped bonnet feeding the red, white and roan Shorthorn calves, tells us more than is immediately obvious. The almond blossom and the Light Sussex hen which is followed by Easter chicks foraging for insects, indicate that the picture was painted in the late spring.

The cottage attached to the Tudor manor house suggests a later addition which was probably occupied by the girl and her daughter, who is seen peering over the wall. It is interesting to note that the thatched roof has gone from the cottage to be replaced with the later Welsh slate, brought now to areas all over England by the railways.

Meyerheim's calves were tended outside rather than in the stall because it had been discovered that the more air they had, the less liable they were to contract tuberculosis, a disease prevalent among cattle until 1875, when the Government established a Veterinary Department.

Robert Mayerheim's time in England was spent in London, and then near Horsham in Sussex, where he died on 16 May 1920.

Feeding the Calves

Courtesy The Priory Gallery

EDMUND GEORGE WARREN

1834-1909

When in 1841 William Henry Fox discovered how a photographic image could be attached permanently to paper, it seemed to many that the art of painting had been dealt a body blow from which it would never recover. In fact, some painters were so convinced that their careers as artists were in danger that they began trying to paint with a photographic realism that they had never tried before, often with a damaging effect on their work. Some, like Edmund Warren, were savagely attacked for painting in this manner, an unfair criticism in his case as he was immensely talented at conveying such realism.

Edmund George Warren was a landscape artist who was born in London in 1834. The son of a well known painter, Henry Warren, he began exhibiting at all the major galleries from the age of eighteen. He quickly attracted the attention of the critics who viewed his work with mixed feelings, amongst them John Ruskin who, while admitting that his paintings were skilfully done, also found them 'mechanical'. Others had nothing but admiration for the photographic realism of his work, especially the way he painted trees with the light filtering through leaves and branches.

The Beech Wood is a typical example of his work. The delicate tracery of the leaves and the sun-dappled patches on the ground where the sun has filtered through, the almost uncanny detail of the tree trunks and the care taken over the autumnal leaves carpeting the woodlands and grass, are all unmistakable hallmarks of Warren's work.

That such woodlands existed for Warren to paint we owe in part to the New Forest Act of 1876, which was created to 'maintain the picturesque quality of the land'. This was a belated move to halt the erosion of the forests of England and Wales, caused by a climate which required the maintaining of household fires throughout much of the year and the ever-increasing demand for arable land. However, by far the most important factor was the need for timber for the naval shipyards, which had caused Britain to become one of the least wooded countries in the world since the end of the Napoleonic Wars. While much of the Crown lands were safeguarded for the public to enjoy the natural beauty of the countryside, and places like Ashdown Forest and Burnham Beeches were indeed conserved for all time, this still did not save the private woodlands in the suburbs of London. Here speculative builders continued to erect their rows of often monstrously ugly houses and so cut great swathes through the suburban woodlands.

The Beech Wood
Courtesy The Priory Gallery

JOHN ABERNETHY LYNAS-GRAY

Exhibited 1897-1928

One of the subjects treated time and time again in Victorian watercolours is a scene of some tranquil country village lined with pretty thatched cottages where bonneted ladies gossip over the fence. Lynas-Gray's *Golden Moments* belongs very much to this genre. Given its title because of the golden glow with which he suffused the watercolour, it seems, at first glance, a highly idealised view with its picturesque house complete with moss growing over the thatch, garden bursting with hollyhocks and sunflowers, and a young woman who has stopped to talk to a friendly puppy. But villages like this did actually exist, and in quite large numbers.

Britain's country villages generally fell into one of two categories: they were either 'closed' or 'open'. The 'closed' villages were those owned by a benevolent local landowner or squire who had built the cottages less as a way of making money than to enhance the surrounds to his own lands and make a kindly gesture to his workers for their loyalty. In exchange, the villagers were expected to give him some form of good-natured loyalty, something almost feudal in concept, but based on good will rather than duress.

In the 'open' village there was no squire, only an absentee landlord or local speculator, who charged exhorbitant rents for the squalid, pokey little cottages, devoid of anything but the basic necessities. The villages were insanitary, overcrowded and inevitably they quickly assumed a run-down air. The only thing to be said in their favour was that the inhabitants owed nobody allegiance. Yet this was a doubtful blessing when they could be evicted at any moment for non-payment of rent. It was, therefore, hardly surprising that, given the choice, most preferred to live in a 'closed' village.

Lynas-Gray was a landscape and genre artist who was born in Oxton, Cheshire in 1869. After studying art in Liverpool and London, he began to show his work in the 1890s and continued to exhibit until as late as 1928. He lived in a number of places, including Yorkshire and Paris. His last known address was in Caernarvonshire.

J. Johnson and A. Greutzner who compiled the invaluable *Dictionary of British Artists 1880-1940* managed to find out where he had exhibited eleven of his pictures. However as he painted over many years this must represent only a fraction of his work. He is an artist who merits rather more attention than has been his lot so far.

Golden Moments

Courtesy The Priory Gallery